Mary Jones, Diane Fellowes-Freeman and Michael Smyth

Cambridge Checkpoint
Science
Skills Builder Workbook

9

CAMBRIDGE
UNIVERSITY PRESS

CAMBRIDGE
UNIVERSITY PRESS

University Printing House, Cambridge CB2 8BS, United Kingdom

One Liberty Plaza, 20th Floor, New York, NY 10006, USA

477 Williamstown Road, Port Melbourne, VIC 3207, Australia

314–321, 3rd Floor, Plot 3, Splendor Forum, Jasola District Centre, New Delhi – 110025, India

79 Anson Road, #06–04/06, Singapore 079906

Cambridge University Press is part of the University of Cambridge.

It furthers the University's mission by disseminating knowledge in the pursuit of
education, learning and research at the highest international levels of excellence.

www.cambridge.org
Information on this title: www.cambridge.org/9781316637241 (Paperback)

© Cambridge University Press 2017

This publication is in copyright. Subject to statutory exception
and to the provisions of relevant collective licensing agreements,
no reproduction of any part may take place without the written
permission of Cambridge University Press.

First published 2017

20 19 18 17 16 15 14 13 12 11 10 9 8

Printed in Great Britain by CPI Group (UK) Ltd, Croydon CR0 4YY

A catalogue record for this publication is available from the British Library

ISBN 978-1-316-63724-1 Paperback

Produced for Cambridge University Press by White-Thomson Publishing
www.wtpub.co.uk
Editor: Izzi Howell
Designer: Clare Nicholas

Cambridge University Press has no responsibility for the persistence or accuracy
of URLs for external or third-party internet websites referred to in this publication,
and does not guarantee that any content on such websites is, or will remain,
accurate or appropriate. Information regarding prices, travel timetables, and other
factual information given in this work is correct at the time of first printing but
Cambridge University Press does not guarantee the accuracy of such information
thereafter.

All Checkpoint-style questions and sample answers within this workbook are
written by the authors.

Acknowledgements

The authors and publishers acknowledge the following sources for photographs:

Cover Pal Hermansen/Steve Bloom Images/Alamy Stock Photo; 5.1 Andrew Lambert
Photography/Science Photo Library

....

NOTICE TO TEACHERS IN THE UK
It is illegal to reproduce any part of this work in material form (including
photocopying and electronic storage) except under the following circumstances:
(i)   where you are abiding by a licence granted to your school or institution by the
       Copyright Licensing Agency;
(ii)   where no such licence exists, or where you wish to exceed the terms of a licence,
       and you have gained the written permission of Cambridge University Press;
(iii) where you are allowed to reproduce without permission under the provisions
       of Chapter 3 of the Copyright, Designs and Patents Act 1988, which covers, for
       example, the reproduction of short passages within certain types of educational
       anthology and reproduction for the purposes of setting examination questions.

Contents

Introduction

Welcome to the Cambridge Checkpoint Science Skills Builder Workbook 9

The Cambridge Checkpoint Science course covers the Cambridge Secondary 1 Science curriculum framework. The course is divided into three stages: 7, 8 and 9.

You should use this Skills Builder Workbook with Coursebook 9 and Workbook 9. This workbook does not cover all of the curriculum framework at stage 9; instead it gives you extra practice in key topics, focusing on those that are the most important, to improve your understanding and confidence.

The tasks will help you with scientific enquiry skills, such as planning investigations, drawing tables to record your results, and plotting graphs.

The workbook will also help you to use your knowledge to work out the answers to new questions.

As you work through the tasks in this Skills Builder Workbook you should find that you get better at these skills.

You could then try to complete some of the exercises in the Checkpoint Science Workbook.

If you get stuck with a task:

Read the question again and look carefully at any diagrams, to find any clues.

Look up any words you do not understand in the glossary at the back of the Checkpoint Science Coursebook, or in your dictionary.

Read through the matching section in the Coursebook. Look carefully at the diagrams there too.

Check the reference section at the back of the Coursebook. There is a lot of useful information there.

Introducing the learners

Nor   Amal   Sam

Anna   Elsa   Jon

1.1 What do plants need for photosynthesis?

This exercise relates to **1.1 Photosynthesis** from the Coursebook.

> In this exercise, you practise making conclusions from results.

Amal puts some aquatic plants (water plants) into different liquids.

One of the liquids is sodium hydrogencarbonate solution. This provides carbon dioxide.

Amal looks to see which plants give off bubbles.

Remember

In photosynthesis, oxygen is given off.

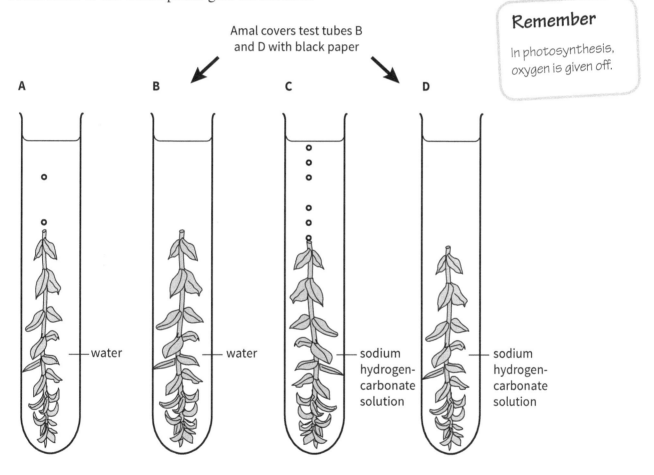

Amal covers test tubes B and D with black paper

1   In which test tubes do the plants have light? ....

2   In which test tubes do the plants have extra carbon dioxide? ....

3   In which test tubes do the plants have water? ....

Amal makes a conclusion from his experiment.

Amal's teacher says: 'You are correct that plants need those three things for photosynthesis.

But your experiment only gives you information about two of them.'

My experiment shows that plants need light, carbon dioxide and water for photosynthesis.

4 Explain how Amal's results show that light is needed for photosynthesis.

....

....

5 Explain how Amal's results show that carbon dioxide is needed for photosynthesis.

....

....

....

6 Explain why Amal's results do **not** show whether plants need water for photosynthesis.

....

....

....

Remember

A conclusion uses **only** the results of the experiment, not other facts that you know.

7 Suggest what Amal could do to test whether water is needed for photosynthesis.

....

....

8 Complete the word equation for photosynthesis.

	+	water	$\longrightarrow$		+	

1.2 Duckweed experiment

This exercise relates to **1.2 Mineral salts for plants** from the Coursebook.

> In this exercise, you practise planning experiments, recording results and making conclusions.

Anna does an experiment to find out if extra nitrate fertiliser helps duckweed plants to grow faster.

She takes five dishes and puts distilled water into them. She labels the dishes **A**, **B**, **C**, **D** and **E**.

She adds one grain of fertiliser to dish **B**, two grains to dish **C**, three grains to dish **D** and four grains to dish **E**.

She puts five duckweed plants into **each** dish.

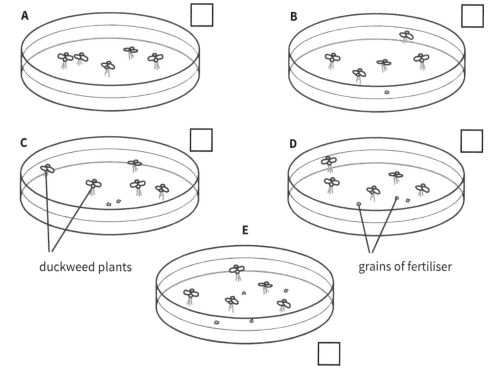

duckweed plants

grains of fertiliser

1 Write the number of grains of fertiliser that Anna puts into each dish in the boxes next to each diagram.

2 Which variable does Anna change in her experiment?
Tick the correct answer.

number of duckweed plants ☐   volume of water ☐   quantity of fertiliser ☐

3 Which variables should Anna keep the same in her experiment?
Tick **all** the correct answers.

number of duckweed plants ☐   quantity of fertiliser ☐   light intensity ☐

volume of water ☐   temperature ☐

After two weeks, Anna counts the number of duckweed plants in each dish.

She writes the results in her notebook.

4 Complete the results chart.

Dish	Number of grains of fertiliser	Number of plants at end of experiment
A	0	5
B		
C		
D		
E		

A 5 plants

B 9 plants

C 10 plants

D 8 plants

E no plants

5 Draw a bar chart to display Anna's results.

Put 'number of grains of fertiliser' on the x-axis.

Put 'number of plants at end of experiment' on the y-axis.

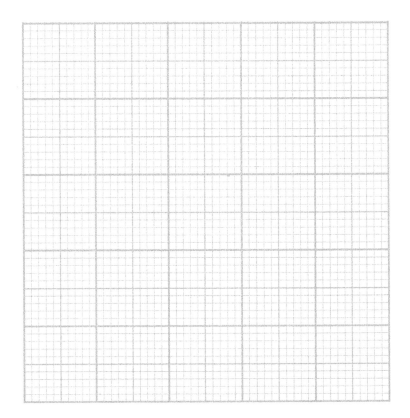

Anna says:

> From my experiment, I conclude that duckweed plants grow more if they have extra nitrate fertiliser. But too much nitrate fertiliser stops them growing.

6 Explain how Anna's results support her conclusion.

....

....

....

....

....

7 How can Anna improve her experiment?
Tick the correct answer.

Use three sets of dishes for each quantity of fertiliser. ☐

Use a different kind of water plant in each dish. ☐

Put each dish in a different temperature. ☐

1.3 Saguaro cactus pollination

This exercise relates to **1.5 Pollination** from the Coursebook.

> In this exercise, you practise finding information in a written passage and using it to answer questions. You also need to use your own knowledge and understanding of pollination.

The saguaro cactus grows in the desert in Arizona, USA. It produces many white flowers at the ends of the branches on its tall stems.

In the cooler times of the year, some of the flowers open each night. Each flower is about 8 cm wide. Its petals form a tube about 10 cm long. There is sweet nectar at the bottom of the tube.

At night, bats are attracted by the sweet smell of the flowers and the shining white petals.

The bats have long tongues. These can reach down to the bottom of the tube, where the nectar is. The bats' heads brush against the anthers. Pollen grains stick to the bats' hair.

When a bat flies to another cactus flower, some of the pollen grains stick to the stigma. The flower has been pollinated.

Each open flower closes the next day, and never opens again.

1 List **two** features of the saguaro flowers that attract bats.

....

2 Suggest why the flowers are produced high up, at the tips of the cactus stems.

....

....

3 Explain how the structure of the flower makes sure that the bats get pollen
on their hair.

....

....

....

4 Suggest why not all of the cactus flowers open on the same night.

....

....

....

5 Pollen grains contain the male gametes of the flowers. Explain how the bats
help the saguaro flowers to reproduce. Use these words in your answer:

pollinate   sexual reproduction

fertilise   male gametes   female gametes

....

....

....

....

....

1.4 Adaptations of fruits for dispersal

This exercise relates to **1.7 Fruits** from the Coursebook.

> In this exercise, you practise explaining your ideas.

Fruits contain seeds.

Fruits have adaptations that help their seeds to be carried far away from the parent plant. This is called dispersal.

The drawings show three different fruits. Two of them are dispersed by animals. One of them is dispersed by the wind.

Fruit A

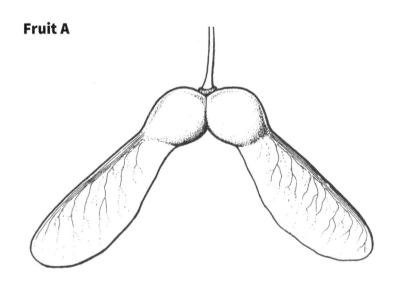

Fruit B

Fruit C

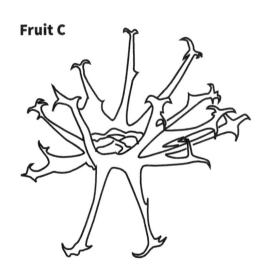

> **Remember**
>
> Study the drawings and think carefully before you write each answer.

1 How is fruit **A** dispersed?
Draw a circle around the correct answer.

by animals / by the wind

Explain your answer.

....

....

....

2 How is fruit **B** dispersed?
Draw a circle around the correct answer.

by animals / by the wind

Explain your answer.

....

....

....

3 How is fruit **C** dispersed?
Draw a circle around the correct answer.

by animals / by the wind

Explain your answer.

....

....

....

4 Explain why it is useful for fruits to be dispersed far away from the parent plant.

....

....

....

....

2.1 Woodlouse experiment

This exercise relates to **2.2 Animal adaptations** from the Coursebook.

> In this exercise, you practise constructing a results chart and interpreting the results of an experiment.

Jon does an experiment to find out if woodlice prefer to be in dark or light places.

He sets up a choice chamber, with one side covered with black paper.

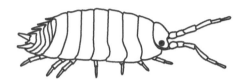

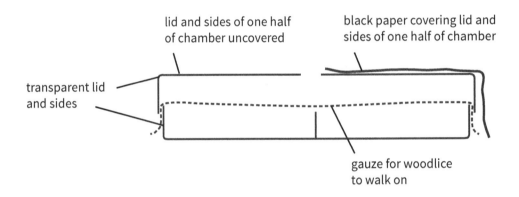

lid and sides of one half of chamber uncovered

black paper covering lid and sides of one half of chamber

transparent lid and sides

gauze for woodlice to walk on

Jon puts ten woodlice into the choice chamber, through a hole in the lid.

Every two minutes, Jon counts how many woodlice he can see in the uncovered side of the chamber.

He does this for 20 minutes.

Here are his results.

6, 10, 7, 4, 3, 3, 2, 0, 0, 0

1 In the space, draw a results chart with two rows.

Write the heading for the first row: 'time / minutes'.

Write the heading for the second row: 'number of woodlice in uncovered side'.

Decide how many columns you need in your results chart.

Then fill in Jon's results.

> **Remember**
>
> Draw your results chart in pencil. Then, if you make a mistake or change your mind, you can rub it out and start again.

2 How many woodlice are in the **covered** side of the container after 20 minutes? ....

3 State a conclusion from Jon's experiment.

....

4 Suggest how the behaviour of the woodlice helps them to survive.

....

....

....

2.2 Building up a food web

This exercise relates to **2.4 Food webs and energy flow** from the Coursebook.

> In this exercise, you practise drawing a food web. You also practise using the correct terms to describe the different organisms in a food web.

The diagram shows a food chain in a sea grass forest in the sea in Central America.

The arrows in the food chain show how energy flows from one organism to the next. This happens when one organism eats another.

In the following questions, your task is to add more organisms to the food chain to make a food web.

humans

queen conch

sea grass

1   Sea urchins eat sea grass.

Add sea urchins to the diagram.

2   Pen shells also eat sea grass.

Add pen shells to the diagram.

3   Phytoplankton are tiny, microscopic plants.
They are eaten by sea urchins, queen conch and pen shells.

Add phytoplankton to the diagram.

4   Helmet snails and stingrays both eat sea urchins and pen shells.

Add helmet snails and stingrays to the diagram.

5   Humans eat helmet snails and stingrays.

Add arrows to the diagram to show this.

6   Which organisms are the producers in your food web?

....

....

7   Name two herbivores in the food web.

....

....

8   Name two carnivores in the food web.

....

....

Remember

Make sure you draw an arrow going **to** the sea urchins **from** their food.

2.3 Decomposers in a compost heap

This exercise relates to **2.5 Decomposers** from the Coursebook.

> In this exercise, you practise using information, and your own knowledge, to answer questions. Some of the information is in words, and some is in a graph.

Many people with gardens like to build a compost heap. This is a collection of waste material that decomposers will gradually break down.

Eventually, the waste material turns into dark, crumbly compost. This is good to add to soil, to help plants to grow well.

The gardener can add paper, cardboard, weeds, vegetable peel and other food waste to the heap. All of these materials are broken down by decomposers.

1 Draw a circle around the items in the list that a gardener should **not** add to a compost heap.

glass   apple peel   newspaper

grass cuttings   metal   plastic

Many of the decomposers are micro-organisms.

The compost heap must be kept moist and have a good air supply.

Turning the materials every few days helps to do this.

2 Imagine you have a sample of material from a compost heap in your school laboratory.

Suggest how you could find out if there are micro-organisms in it.

....

....

....

....

3 Explain why it is important to keep a compost heap moist and with a good air supply. (Think about the micro-organisms.)

....

....

Chemical reactions take place as the decomposers break down the material in the compost heap. Some of these reactions release heat energy.

The graph shows the temperature in a compost heap over a period of 17 days.

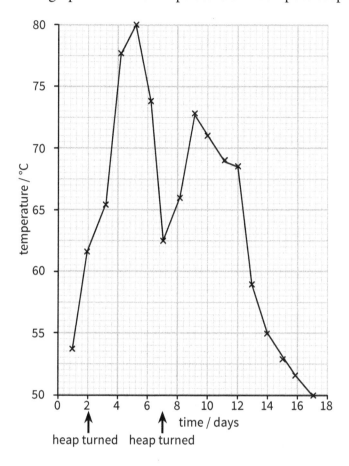

4 What is the temperature on day 1? ....

5 What is the highest temperature that is reached? ....

6 Suggest why the temperature rises between day 7 and day 9.

....

....

....

7 Suggest why the temperature gradually falls after day 9.

....

....

....

3.1 Using a key to identify fish

This exercise relates to **3.1 Keys** from the Coursebook.

> In this exercise, you practise using a key to identify an animal.

The diagrams show four fish.

A

B

C

D

In the questions, you will use this key to find out the name of each fish.

1 **a** It has a row of gill slits .... go to step 2

  b No gill slits can be seen .... go to step 3

2 **a** Its eye is above the front end of its mouth .... basking shark

  b Its eye is above the back end of its mouth .... Greenland shark

3 **a** It has long spines on its top fin .... John Dory

  b It has short spines on its top fin............................sea bream

1 Start with fish **A**.

Look at step 1 in the key. Read descriptions 1a and 1b.

a Which description fits fish **A**? ....

The key tells you which step to go to next.

Go to this step, and choose which description fits fish **A**.

b What is the name of fish **A**? ....

2 Now work through the key to identify fish **B**.

a Which description in step 1 fits fish **B**? ....

Go to the next step.

b What is the name of fish **B**? ....

3 Now work through the key again to identify fish **C**.

What is the name of fish **C**? ....

4 Identify fish **D**. ....

3.2 Growing rice in Indonesia

This exercise relates to **3.5 Selective breeding** from the Coursebook.

> In this exercise, you practise finding information in graphs. You also make sure that you understand how selective breeding is carried out.

Rice is an important food crop in Indonesia.

As the population of Indonesia increases, the quantity of rice that is produced also increases.

One way of increasing the quantity of rice is to use more fertiliser.

The graph shows the change in the mass of fertiliser used for growing rice in Indonesia between 1960 and 2009.

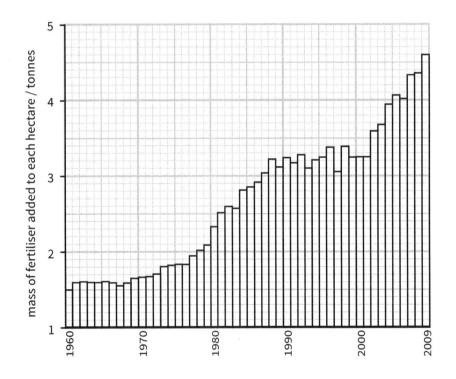

Remember

Give the unit with your answer.

1 How much fertiliser was used for growing rice in 1961? ....

2 How much fertiliser was used for growing rice in 2010? ....

3 Calculate the increase in the mass of fertiliser used for growing rice between 1960 and 2009.

....

4 Explain why using fertiliser can help to produce larger quantities of rice.

....

....

....

The amount of rice produced from a crop is called the yield.

Another way of increasing the yield is to use selective breeding.

In Indonesia, selective breeding has given new varieties of rice plant with higher yields. This means that farmers can harvest more rice from the same area of land.

This graph shows the change in the mass of rice harvested from one hectare of land between 1960 and 2009.

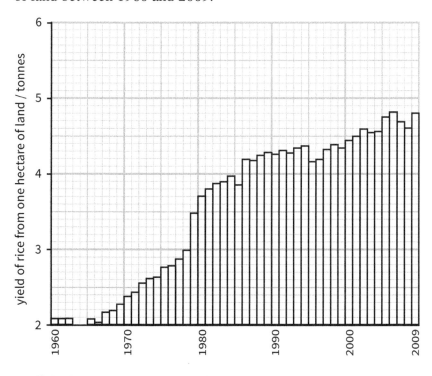

5 Calculate how much more rice was harvested from one hectare of land in 2009, than in 1960.

Show your working.

Go through the same steps that you did to answer questions 1, 2 and 3.

....

....

....

6 The sentences below describe how the scientists in Indonesia used selective breeding to produce new varieties of rice plant.

The sentences are in the wrong order.

Write a number next to each sentence to show the correct order. The first number has been done for you.

A They repeated the breeding process with the new, high-yielding plants. ☐

B They planted the seeds and waited for them to grow into new rice plants. ☐

C The scientists took pollen from the flowers of one high-yielding rice plant, and put it onto the stigmas of the flowers of a different kind of high-yielding rice plant. ☐ 1

D They waited for the rice plant to produce seeds. ☐

E They did this again and again for many years. ☐

F They selected the new plants that had the highest yield. ☐

3.3 Blue-tailed lizards

This exercise relates to **3.4 More about inheritance** and **3.6 Natural selection** from the Coursebook.

> In this exercise, you improve your understanding of how natural selection works.

When a lizard is attacked by a predator, the lizard's tail falls off.

The tail squirms violently, attracting the attention of the predator.

While the predator is attacking the tail, the lizard runs off and hides. It grows a new tail.

Some lizards have blue tails. Snakes are especially good at seeing the colour blue.

In places where snakes are the main predators of lizards, the lizards are more likely to have blue tails.

blue

1 The lizard's genes determine the colour of its tail.

Which part of the lizard's cells contains genes?

cell membrane ☐   cytoplasm ☐   nucleus ☐

2 Two parent lizards with blue tails pass on their genes for blue tails to their offspring.

What is the name for this process?

DNA ☐   inheritance ☐   variation ☐

3 A population of lizards lives on an island where there are no snakes. Some of the lizards have brown tails and some have blue tails.

Some snakes arrive on the island.

Explain why the lizards with brown tails are more likely to be eaten by snakes than the lizards with blue tails.

....

....

4 In the next generation, more lizards are born with blue tails than with brown tails. Tick the correct explanation.

The lizards change their tail colour so that they will not be eaten by snakes. ☐

More parent lizards with blue tails survive, so they are the ones that reproduce. They pass on their genes for blue tails to their offspring. ☐

The lizards learn that it is safer to have a blue tail, so they have offspring with blue tails. ☐

3.4 Camouflaged caterpillars

This exercise relates to **3.7 Natural selection in action** from the Coursebook.

> In this exercise, you make sure that you understand how natural selection works. You also think about designing good experiments.

Nor and Elsa are looking at caterpillars.

They find out that a species of moth usually has green caterpillars, but sometimes has yellow caterpillars.

The girls have an idea that they decide to test:

In a grassy area, green caterpillars are less likely to be found by a predator than yellow caterpillars.

Nor and Elsa use pieces of spiral-shaped pasta to represent caterpillars. They make 100 'caterpillars'.

They colour 50 of the 'caterpillars' green, and 50 yellow.

They put all the coloured pasta pieces together in a bucket and shake them up.

The girls then spread the pasta pieces over a grassy area outside the classroom.

Then they ask Jon to pick up the first 20 pasta caterpillars he can find.

1 What measurements or observations should the girls make to test their idea?
   Tick the correct answer.

   the time taken for Jon to find 20 caterpillars ☐

   how many green caterpillars and how many yellow caterpillars Jon picks up ☐

   which hand Jon uses to pick up the caterpillars ☐

2 The girls decide that they need more results, so that they can make a
   reliable conclusion. What should they do next?
   Tick the correct answer.

   Repeat the experiment five times with the same caterpillars, using five
   different students to collect them. ☐

   Repeat the experiment using 25 green caterpillars and 75 yellow caterpillars. ☐

   Repeat the experiment using 50 blue caterpillars and 50 red caterpillars. ☐

3 Nor and Elsa think about why the real caterpillars of the moth are more likely
   to be green than yellow, when living in a grassy area.

   They write five sentences to explain how natural selection could make this
   happen. Their sentences are here but in the wrong order.

   Write a number next to each sentence to show the correct order. The first
   number has been written for you.

   A The adult moths mate and lay fertilised eggs. ☐

   B So adult moths are more likely to contain genes for producing green
     caterpillars than for producing yellow caterpillars. ☐

   C So more green caterpillars hatch out of the eggs than yellow caterpillars. ☐

   D Green caterpillars are more likely to survive and grow up into adult moths. 1

   E The fertilised eggs are more likely to contain genes for producing green
     caterpillars than for producing yellow caterpillars. ☐

4.1 What is an atom made of?

This exercise relates to **4.1 The structure of the atom** from the Coursebook.

> In this exercise, you label the structure of an atom.

All atoms are made up of protons,
neutrons and electrons.

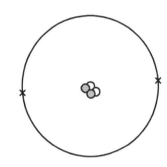

1 Label the diagram of the structure of an atom. Use the labels given here.

proton   neutron   electron   nucleus of atom   path of electrons

Remember that protons
and neutrons are in the
middle of the atom.

Remember to keep your
writing straight and use
a ruler for labelling lines.

2 What is in the white area inside the circle in the diagram? Label it.

3 Tick the statements that are correct.

Electrons have less mass than protons. ☐

Protons have a negative electrical charge. ☐

Electrons have a negative electrical charge. ☐

Neutrons have an electrical charge. ☐

Neutrons have more mass than electrons. ☐

Electrons are found in the nucleus of the atom. ☐

4.2 How many protons and neutrons are in an atom?

This exercise relates to **4.2 More about the structure of the atom** from the Coursebook.

> In this exercise, you work out the structure of atoms from information in the Periodic Table.

The atoms of one element are different from the atoms of all other elements.

They have a different atomic number and a different mass number.

metals								1 H hydrogen 1									2 He helium 4
non-metals																	
3 Li lithium 7	4 Be beryllium 9											5 B boron 11	6 C carbon 12	7 N nitrogen 14	8 O oxygen 16	9 F fluorine 19	10 Ne neon 20
11 Na sodium 23	12 Mg magnesium 24											13 Al aluminium 27	14 Si silicon 28	15 P phosphorus 31	16 S sulfur 32	17 Cl chlorine 35	18 Ar argon 40
19 K potassium 39	20 Ca calcium 40																

1 What is the atomic number for magnesium? ....

2 What is the mass number for nitrogen? ....

3 Which element has the atomic number 13? ....

4 Which element has the mass number 20? ....

> **Remember**
>
> The smaller number is the atomic number.
>
> The larger number is the mass number.

Atoms of different elements have different numbers of protons, neutrons and electrons.

Look at this example.

Atomic number = 3

Mass number = 7

Number of protons = 3

Number of neutrons = 7 − 3 = 4

Number of electrons = 3 (always the same as number of protons)

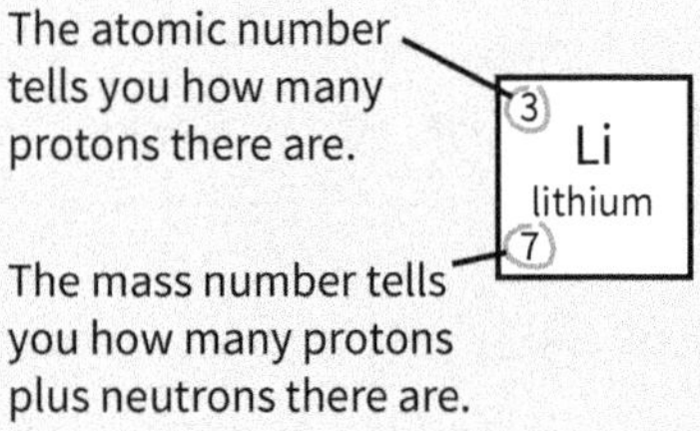

The atomic number tells you how many protons there are.

③ Li
lithium
⑦

The mass number tells you how many protons plus neutrons there are.

5 Complete these numbers for a carbon atom:

6 C
carbon
12

Atomic number = ...

Mass number = ...

Number of protons = ...

Number of neutrons = ...

Number of electrons = ...

6 Complete these numbers for a boron atom:

5 B
boron
11

Atomic number = ...

Mass number = ...

Number of protons = ...

Number of neutrons = ...

Number of electrons = ...

4.3 Elements in the same group

This exercise relates to **4.3 Trends in Group 1** from the Coursebook.

> In this exercise, you compare the structure of atoms in Group 1.

Elements in the same group are similar.

Lithium, sodium and potassium are elements in Group 1.
They are all metals.

| 3 Li lithium 7 |
| 11 Na sodium 23 |
| 19 K potassium 39 |

1 What can you say about the number of protons in these three metals, as you look down the group?

....

2 What can you say about the mass number of these three metals, as you look down the group?

....

Lithium has electrons arranged in two shells.

It has two electrons in the first (inner) shell, and one electron in the second (outer) shell.

This is shown as 2,1. It is called the electronic structure.

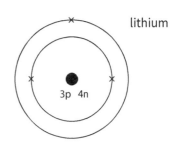
lithium
3p 4n

3 This diagram shows the structure of a sodium atom. Complete these numbers for sodium:

Atomic number = ...

Mass number = ...

Number of protons = ...

Number of neutrons = ...

Number of electrons = ...

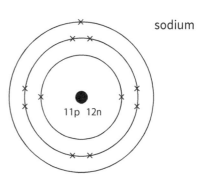
sodium
11p 12n

4 Write the electronic structure of sodium. ……………………………

5 What is similar about the structures of an atom of lithium and an atom of sodium?

………

………

6 This diagram shows the structure of a potassium atom. Complete these numbers for potassium:

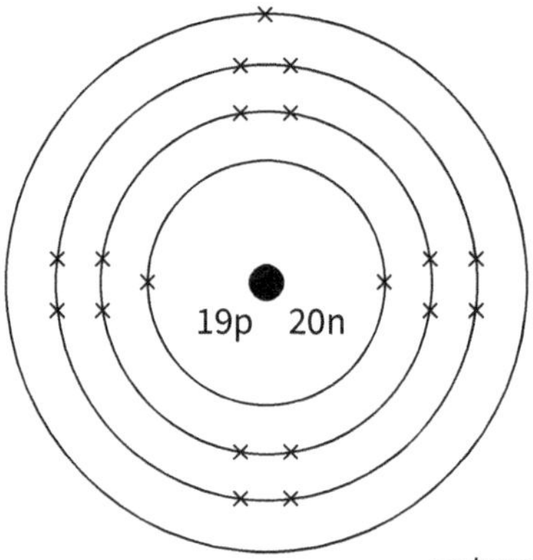

Atomic number = ……………………………

Mass number = ……………………………

Number of protons = ……………………………

Number of neutrons = ……………………………

Number of electrons = ……………………………

potassium

7 Write the electronic structure of potassium. ……………………………

8 Compare the structure of the atoms of these three metals of Group 1. What is similar about their structure?

………

………

………

9 What is different about the three atoms? Try to state two differences.

………

………

………

………

5.1 What happens when things burn?

This exercise relates to **5.1 Burning** from the Coursebook.

> In this exercise, you identify the energy changes and the chemical changes when something burns.

When fuel burns, energy is given out.

In a fire, the chemical energy in the fuel is changed to other types of energy when the fuel burns.

1 Name the types of energy given out.

....

....

This is the word equation for the burning of carbon in oxygen:

 carbon   +   oxygen   ⟶   carbon dioxide

2 Colour the atoms of carbon grey, and the atoms of oxygen red.

3 What is the product in this reaction?

....

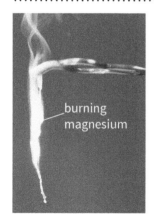

burning magnesium

A reaction that gives out energy is called an exothermic reaction.

Burning magnesium gives out energy.

4 Write the word equation for burning magnesium in oxygen.

....

....

5 State another reaction that is exothermic.

....

....

> Think about when your teacher put some metals in water. There are some reactions that produce a bang or a flame.

5.2 Investigating an exothermic reaction

This exercise relates to **5.2 More exothermic reactions** from the Coursebook.

In this exercise, you identify variables and interpret results.

Nor and Sam are measuring the temperature rise in a reaction between magnesium ribbon and hydrochloric acid.

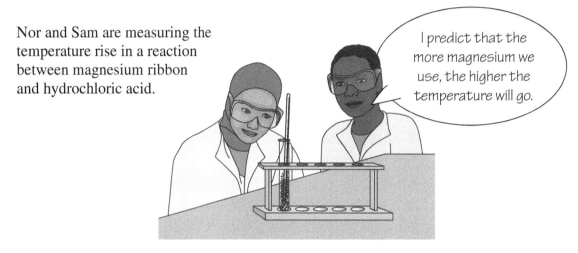

I predict that the more magnesium we use, the higher the temperature will go.

They want to find out if using a longer piece of magnesium ribbon makes the temperature rise higher.

1 What is the **independent variable** in this investigation? ....

2 What is the **dependent variable**? ....

3 What are the **control variables**? State at least two.

....

....

Nor and Sam do some tests first, to find out how much they must change the length of magnesium each time. This change in variable is called the **interval**.

4 Here are the results of these tests. Complete the table.

Length of ribbon / cm	Start temperature / °C	End temperature / °C	Temperature change / °C
0.5	19	36	
1.0	19	36	
1.5	19	36.5	

5 Describe what the results show.

....

....

6 Do Sam and Nor have enough data to say that Sam's prediction is correct? ....
Explain your answer.

....

....

7 What is the interval in length they used? ....

8 Should they use a **larger** or **smaller** interval for the main investigation? ....
Explain why.

....

....

9 Suggest how many different lengths of magnesium ribbon they should use. ....

Some of the heat is lost to the surroundings

heat loss

10 How can Nor and Sam reduce the heat loss from the test tube?

....

11 Explain how they can make their results **reliable**.

....

....

5.3 Energy changes

This exercise relates to **5.4 Exothermic or endothermic?** from the Coursebook.

> In this exercise, you practise identifying whether reactions are exothermic or endothermic.

1 For each of the reactions in the table, write **exothermic** or **endothermic**.

> **Remember**
> - In an **exothermic** reaction, heat energy is given out to the environment and the reaction temperature **increases**.
> - In an **endothermic** reaction, heat energy is taken in from the environment and the reaction temperature **decreases**.

Reaction	Start temperature / °C	Final temperature / °C	Exothermic or endothermic?
A	21	45	
B	18	22	
C	19	16	
D	18	20	

2 Sherbet sweets react with the water in your mouth to give a cool, fizzy feeling.

Is this an endothermic reaction or an exothermic reaction?

....

3 Self-heating cans use a chemical reaction to warm the food inside.

Is this an endothermic reaction or an exothermic reaction?

....

4 When you put an ice pack from the freezer onto an injury, it takes the heat away from the injured area.

This is called an endothermic **process** not an endothermic **reaction**.

Suggest why this is.

....

....

5 Explain the endothermic process of ice melting, in terms of the particles in the ice.

Make sure you write about the energy changes.

....

....

....

....

....

....

6.1 Investigating reactivity

This exercise relates to **6.3 Reactions of metals with dilute acid** from the Coursebook.

> In this exercise, you practise identifying variables in an investigation.

Amal and Jon are investigating the reaction of different metals with acid.

They have four metals, **A**, **B**, **C** and **D**. They want to compare how reactive these are.

They place a piece of each metal into a test tube of dilute hydrochloric acid. They watch to see how many bubbles it produces.

1 The result for one metal in the test above cannot be compared with the others. Explain why.

....

....

2 What have Jon and Amal done to keep safe?

....

Two other pairs of students do the same investigation. Anna and Nor set it up as shown here.

Anna's and Nor's test

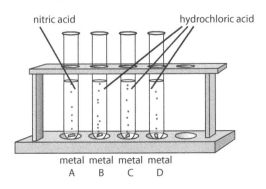

3 Why is Anna's and Nor's test **not** a fair test?

....

....

4 This is Sam's and Elsa's set up. Is it a fair test? Explain your answer.

Sam's and Elsa's test

hydrochloric acid

metal metal metal metal
A   B   C   D

....

....

5 Make a new plan for the investigation. Use the questions below and on the next page to guide you.

a What are you trying to find out?

....

....

b What will you change in the investigation?

....

c What will you measure or observe in the investigation?

....

d Which variables will you keep the same in the investigation? State at least three.

....

....

....

e Describe how you will carry out this investigation.

....

....

....

....

....

....

....

....

....

....

....

f What do you expect to observe?

....

....

g What will this tell you?

....

....

6 Complete the word equation for the reaction between magnesium and hydrochloric acid.

magnesium + hydrochloric $\longrightarrow$ .... + hydrogen
acid

....

7 Which **salt** is produced when **zinc** reacts with hydrochloric acid?

....

> **Remember**
>
> When a metal reacts with an acid, the products are a salt and hydrogen.

6.2 Using the reactivity series

This exercise relates to **6.4 The reactivity series** from the Coursebook.

> In this exercise, you use the information from the reactivity series to make some predictions.

The diagram shows the reactivity series of metals.

1 Sodium burns brightly when heated, and forms an oxide.

   Does magnesium react **more vigorously** or **less vigorously** than sodium?

   ....

   ....

2 Copper reacts very slowly when heated.

   Suggest how silver reacts when heated.

   ....

   ....

3 Lead reacts very slowly with dilute acid.

   How do you expect iron to react with dilute acid, compared with lead?

   ....

   ....

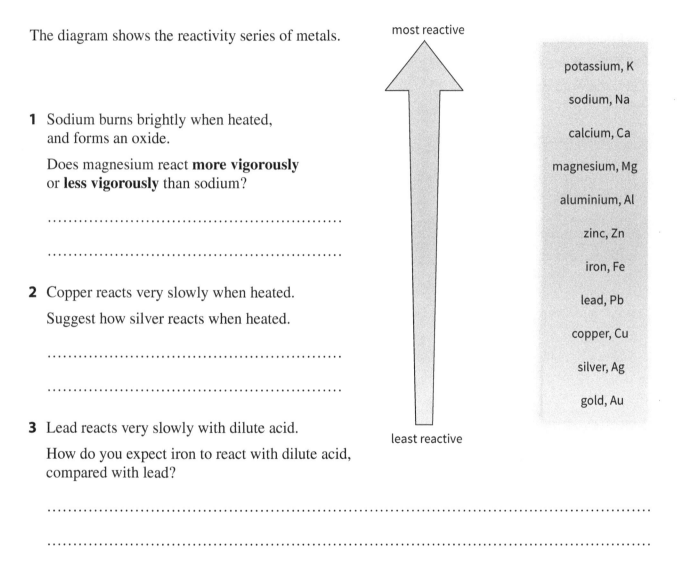

most reactive

potassium, K

sodium, Na

calcium, Ca

magnesium, Mg

aluminium, Al

zinc, Zn

iron, Fe

lead, Pb

copper, Cu

silver, Ag

gold, Au

least reactive

6.3 Metals and metal salts

This exercise relates to **6.5 Displacement reactions** and **6.6 Using displacement reactions** from the Coursebook.

> In this exercise, you identify metals that can displace other metals from their salts.

If an iron nail is put in a solution of copper sulfate, there is a reaction.

This is the word equation:

$$\text{copper sulfate} \ + \ \text{iron} \longrightarrow \text{iron sulfate} \ + \text{copper}$$

Iron is **more reactive** than copper, so it 'pushes out' or **displaces** the copper from the sulfate.

1 If you put a copper nail in a solution of iron sulfate, will there be a displacement reaction?

....

Explain your answer.

....

....

2 Suggest a metal that **cannot** displace the copper in a solution of copper sulfate.

....

Look at the reactivity series from the last exercise to help you with questions 2 to 5.

3 Metal X **displaces lead** in a solution of lead chloride.

Metal X **does not displace zinc** in a solution of zinc chloride.

Suggest which metal X could be. ....

4 Look at these possible reactions. Write **yes** next to those that will happen, and **no** next to those that will not.

   a zinc and copper sulfate, to give copper ....

   b lead and magnesium chloride, to give magnesium ....

   c copper and aluminium chloride, to give aluminium ....

   d zinc and iron chloride, to give iron ....

   e iron and lead chloride, to give lead ....

5 Write the word equation for the reaction between magnesium and zinc chloride.

               +   ⟶   +

Unit 7 Salts

7.1 Which acid is used to make which salt?

This exercise relates to **7.1 What is a salt?** from the Coursebook.

> In this exercise, you identify which acid is used to produce a salt. Then you identify a salt from its formula.

1 Link the name of the acid with its formula, and with the name of the salt it produces.
Draw lines to link the boxes. Use a ruler.

Acid	Formula	Salt
hydrochloric acid	HNO_3	sulfates
sulfuric acid	HCl	nitrates
nitric acid	H_2SO_4	chlorides

2 The following compounds are all salts of sodium.

For each one, state which acid is used to make the salt.

Sodium chloride ……………………………………………

Sodium nitrate ……………………………………………

Sodium sulfate ……………………………………………

3 Write the name of the salt next to its formula.

NaCl ……………………………………………

$CuSO_4$ ……………………………………………

$CuCl_2$ ……………………………………………

KNO_3 ……………………………………………

4 Citric acid is found in fruit. What are salts of this acid called?

……………………………………………………………………

7.2 Preparing copper chloride

This exercise relates to **7.3 Metal carbonates and acids** from the Coursebook.

> In this exercise, you explain the steps in the formation of a salt.
> You also consider safety precautions needed when preparing a salt.

Sam and Elsa are preparing the salt copper chloride.

Sam pours some hydrochloric acid into a beaker.
Then Elsa adds some copper carbonate.

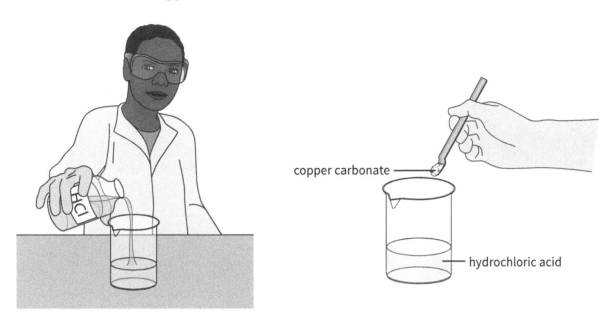

copper carbonate

hydrochloric acid

1 What happens when Elsa adds the copper carbonate to the acid?

....

....

Elsa adds more and more copper carbonate until there is no more reaction.

There is some unreacted copper carbonate left in the beaker.

Sam filters the mixture.

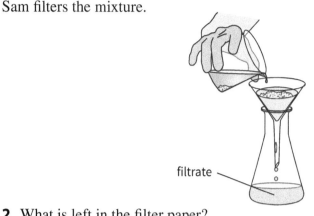

filtrate

2 What is left in the filter paper?

....

3 The filtrate passes through the filter paper into the flask. What is this liquid?

....

4 Next, Sam and Elsa want to produce crystals of the salt. What must they do?

....

....

5 Why must they be very careful when they carry out this step?

....

....

6 What should they do to reduce the hazard?

....

....

....

7 Write the word equation for this reaction.

+   ⟶   +

Remember

Think: What is reacting with what? What is the product?

7.3 Preparing potassium chloride

This exercise relates to **7.4 Forming salts by neutralisation** from the Coursebook.

> In this exercise, you describe the steps needed in some practical work to produce a salt from an acid and an alkali.

Anna and Jon want to prepare the salt potassium chloride, using potassium hydroxide and hydrochloric acid.

1 For the first step in this process, Jon and Anna put 20 cm³ of potassium hydroxide in a beaker. They use the acid to neutralise it.

List the equipment that they need for this first step.

....

....

....

....

....

2 Describe the method for carrying out this step. Include safety precautions.

....

....

....

....

....

....

....

....

3 How will Jon and Anna know when the potassium hydroxide is neutralised?

....

....

4 When the potassium hydroxide is neutralised, Anna and Jon have a coloured solution.

How do they remove the colour, so that the crystals of potassium chloride they prepare are pure?

....

....

....

5 Write the word equation for the neutralisation reaction.

+ $\longrightarrow$ +

> **Remember**
>
> The general equation for a neutralisation reaction is
>
> acid + alkali ⟶ salt + water

6 What is an **alkali**?

....

....

You may need to look up the meaning in the Coursebook.

7 Potassium hydroxide is an alkali. Give an example of another alkali.

....

8 What is a base?

....

9 Potassium oxide is a base. Give an example of another base.

....

8.1 Investigating the reaction of calcium carbonate with an acid

This exercise relates to **8.1 Measuring the rate of reaction** from the Coursebook.

> In this exercise, you plot a graph of the volume of product obtained against time and interpret this.

Anna and Nor investigate the reaction of calcium carbonate with sulfuric acid.

They use the apparatus shown here to measure the total volume of gas given off every 20 seconds.

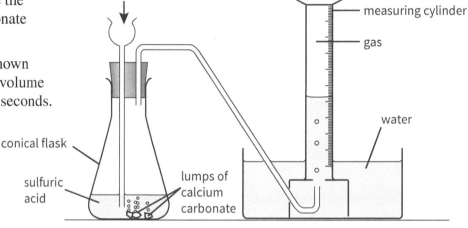

1 What is the name of the gas given off in the reaction?

....

Here are the girls' results.

Time / seconds	Total volume of gas produced / cm³
0	0
20	200
40	350
60	450
80	520
100	560
120	580
140	580
160	580

2 Plot a graph of these results.

Time goes on the x-axis.

Volume goes on the y-axis.

Remember

Use most of the graph grid. Check your scales carefully.

3 Describe what the graph shows.

....

....

....

....

4 Suggest why no gas is given off after 120 seconds.

....

....

8.2 Showing the change in rate of reaction on a graph

This exercise relates to **8.2 Changes in the rate of reaction** from the Coursebook.

> In this exercise, you have more practice at interpreting a graph showing rate of reaction.

Magnesium ribbon is added to hydrochloric acid.

The gas hydrogen is given off. This is collected and its volume measured in a syringe.

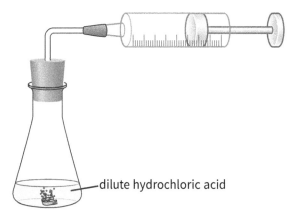

This graph shows the volume of gas collected as time progresses. It shows us the **rate of reaction** between magnesium ribbon and hydrochloric acid.

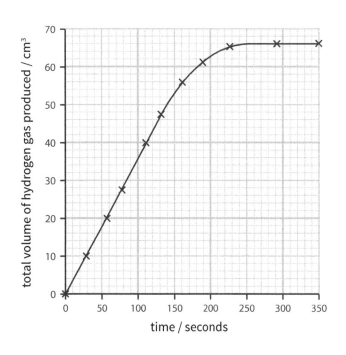

> ### Remember
>
> The **slope** of the line on the graph tells you the rate of reaction.
>
> The **steeper** the line, the faster the reaction.

1 Tick the correct answer. The greatest rate of reaction is:

between 0 seconds and 100 seconds ☐

between 150 seconds and 250 seconds ☐

between 250 seconds and 350 seconds ☐

2 Tick the correct answer. The lowest rate of reaction is between:

between 0 seconds and 100 seconds ☐

between 150 seconds and 250 seconds ☐

between 250 seconds and 350 seconds ☐

3 How much hydrogen gas is produced between 0 seconds and 100 seconds?

....

4 Calculate how much hydrogen gas is produced between 150 seconds and 250 seconds.

....

....

....

Read the volume of hydrogen gas produced from the scale on the graph.

8.3 Explaining changes in the rate of reaction

This exercise relates to **8.4 Temperature and the rate of reaction** from the Coursebook.

> In this exercise, you use particle theory to explain changes in the rate of reaction.

For a reaction to take place, particles of the reactants must collide with enough energy to react with each other.

When there are many particles, the particles collide with each other more often.

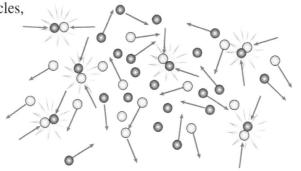

Remember

The **reactants** are the chemicals you have at the start of the reaction.

The **products** are the chemicals formed after the reaction is complete.

1 Explain the following, using particle theory and ideas about collisions.

   a The rate of reaction at the start of a reaction is high.

    ....

    ....

    ....

   b The rate of reaction slows down after a time.

    ....

    ....

    ....

2 Explain, using the same ideas, why increasing the temperature increases the rate of reaction.

> When particles have more energy, they move more quickly.

....

....

....

....

9.1 Density and mass

This exercise relates to **9.1 The idea of density** from the Coursebook.

> In this exercise, you explore the difference between mass and density.

Mass is the **quantity of matter**, or of particles, in an object.
It is measured in units such as grams (g) or kilograms (kg).

Density is the **mass of a known volume** of that object.
It is measured in units such as grams per cubic centimetre (g/cm³)
or kilograms per cubic metre (kg/m³).

Look at these examples.

The block of iron in diagram **A** has the **same mass** as the block of wood.

A

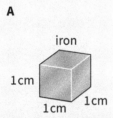
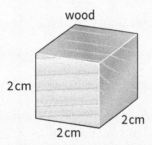

Both blocks have a mass of 8 g, but the block of iron is smaller.

This means that the **density of iron is greater** than that of wood.

Now look at diagram **B**. The block of iron and the block of wood are the same size – they have the **same volume**.

B

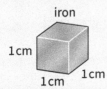
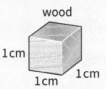

Which block has the greater mass?

The answer is the iron, because its **density is greater** than the wood, so the same volume will have more mass.

1 The diagram shows a block of plastic and a block of lead.

Both blocks have the **same volume**.

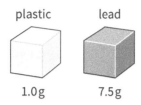

plastic   lead

1.0g   7.5g

Which material is more dense? ....

2 The diagram shows a block of ice and a block of stone.

Both blocks have the **same mass**.

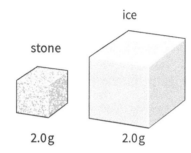

ice

stone

2.0g   2.0g

Which material is more dense? ....

> **Remember**
>
> When comparing two objects of different density:
>
> • when they have the **same volume**, the **more dense** one has **more mass**
>
> • when they have the **same mass**, the **more dense** one has **smaller volume**.

This table shows the mass of 1 cm³ of some materials. Use the data in the table to answer questions 3, 4 and 5.

Material	Mass of 1 cm³ of material / g
plastic	0.93
water	1.00
sponge	0.24
wood	0.93
brick	2.31

3 Name the material from the table that has the lowest density. ....

4 Name the material from the table that is more dense than water. ....

5 If samples of all the materials in the table had the same mass, which one would have the biggest volume?

....

6 Which state of matter usually has the lowest density?
Tick one box.

solid ☐

liquid ☐

gas ☐

9.2 Measuring volumes

This exercise relates to **9.2 Measuring density** from the Coursebook.

> In this exercise, you work out the volumes of some different objects. First you look at objects with regular shapes, then you look at objects with irregular shapes.

Look at this example of a regular shape.

The block of wood in the diagram has a regular shape.

The lengths of its sides have been measured.

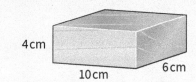

We work out the volume of the block by **multiplying** the lengths of the sides:

$10 \times 6 \times 4 = 240 \, cm^3$

The unit is cm^3 because the lengths of the sides are in cm.

It does **not** matter in what order you multiply the sides.

Try multiplying the numbers in a different order. You should get the same answer.

Sam has a block of metal.

Sam wants to measure the lengths of the three sides.

1 What piece of equipment should he use? ....

2 He finds that the lengths of the sides are 5 cm, 7 cm and 3 cm.

   Work out the volume of the block. Show your working.

............cm^3

3 The lengths of the sides of some different blocks are given.

Calculate the volume of each block.

a 2 cm, 20 cm, 5 cm

..............cm³

b 3.5 cm, 2.8 cm, 4.5 cm

..............cm³

> **Remember**
>
> To work out the volume of a regular brick-shaped object, multiply the lengths of the three sides together, in any order.

Now look at this example of an irregular shape.

This piece of rock has an irregular shape.

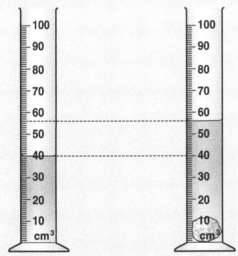

It is placed into a measuring cylinder containing 40 cm³ water.

The water goes up to the 56 cm³ mark.

The volume of the piece of rock is:

56 − 40 = 16 cm³

The unit is cm³ because the measuring cylinder measures in cm³.

4 Elsa has a lump of modelling clay. She wants to measure its volume.

Write the numbers 2, 3 and 4 in the boxes to show the order that Elsa should carry out each step.

Work out the increase in volume.

Put 50 cm³ of water in a 100 cm³ measuring cylinder. | 1 |

Put the modelling clay into the water in the measuring cylinder.

Record the new volume in the measuring cylinder.

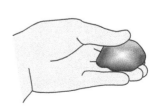

5 Some irregular objects have been placed in measuring cylinders to work out their volumes.

Write down the volume of each object in the space provided.

Remember

To work out the volume of an irregular object, find the **change** in volume of water that it causes.

a

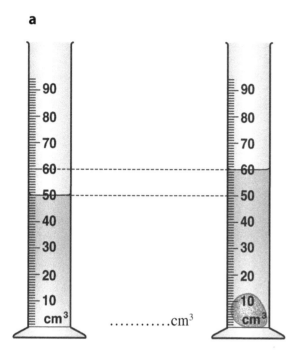

.............cm³

b

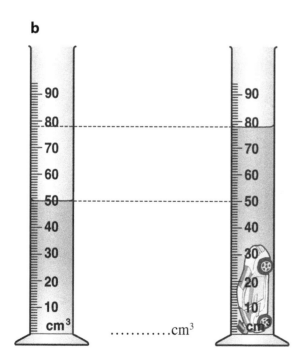

.............cm³

c

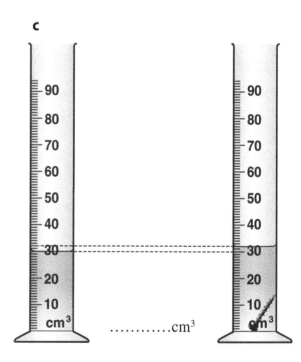

.............cm³

9.3 Calculating the density

This exercise relates to **9.3 Density calculations** from the Coursebook.

> In this exercise, you consider how to measure mass, and then calculate the density of some materials.

Density is worked out using the formula:

$$\textbf{density} = \frac{\textbf{mass}}{\textbf{volume}}$$

Look at this example.

A small block of aluminium has a mass of 27 g.

It has a volume of 10 cm³.

Calculate the density of the aluminium.

Use the formula to divide the mass, 27 g, by the volume, 10 cm³.

$27 \div 10 = 2.7 \, \text{g/cm}^3$

The unit is **g/cm³** because mass is in **g** and volume is in **cm³**.

You do not always divide a larger number by a smaller one. The answer to a density question can be less than 1.

1 The masses and volumes of some objects are given.

Work out the density of each object. Show your working each time.

a mass = 100 g, volume = 10 cm³

…………g/cm³

b mass = 45 g, volume = 9 cm³

…………g/cm³

c mass = 20 g, volume = 80 cm³

…………g/cm³

9.4 Force and pressure

This exercise relates to **9.4 Pressure** from the Coursebook.

> In this exercise, you make some predictions about pressure.

Pressure is the force that acts over a certain area when objects push together.

A large force acting on a small area gives large pressure.

As the **area increases**, with the same force, the **pressure decreases**.

Look at this example.

A thumb tack has two ends.

This end has a **large area** so a **small pressure** acts on your thumb. It does not hurt your thumb.

This end has a **small area** so a **large pressure** acts on the wall. It goes into the wall easily.

Remember

- Sharp, pointed objects have a small area so produce a large pressure.
- Wide, flat objects have a large area so produce a small pressure.
- As the pushing force increases, the pressure increases.

1 Jon has a flag pole made from wood. He wants to push the flag pole into the ground.

What type of statement is Jon making?
Tick **one** box.

a conclusion ☐

an observation ☐

a plan ☐

a prediction ☐

> I think if I push with a larger force, it will go further into the ground.

2 Jon pushes on some different flag poles with a force of 200 N.

Which of these flag poles will go into the ground furthest?

Write A, B, C or D. …………

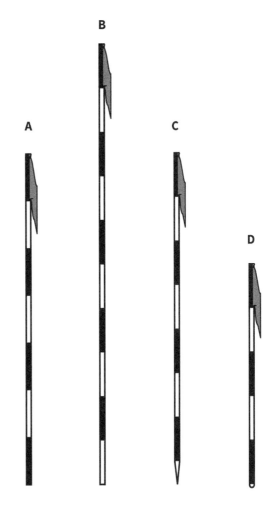

3 Elsa's mother is going outside in soft snow.

She can choose between four pairs of shoes.

Which shoes should she wear so she does **not** sink in soft snow?
Tick **one** box.

9.5 Pressure in air and water

This exercise relates to **9.6 Pressure in gases and liquids** from the Coursebook.

> In this exercise, you make predictions about the effects of pressure in air and in water.

The pressure in air is greatest at sea level and lowest very high up in the atmosphere.

The diagram shows Sam, a bird, a cloud and an aeroplane.

1 Which of these has the **lowest** air pressure around it/him? Draw a circle around **one** answer.

Sam   the bird   the cloud   the aeroplane

The pressure in water is greatest at the deepest part and lowest near the water surface.

2 Look at the information about the different types of fish.

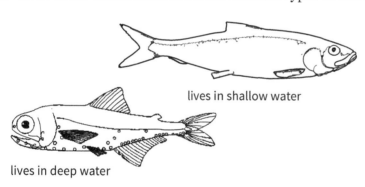

lives in shallow water

lives in deep water

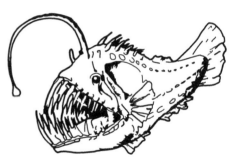

lives in deep water

Match each type of fish to the pressure where it is adapted to live. Draw **one** line from each fish.

Type of fish	Pressure where it is adapted to live
	low pressure
	high pressure

The diagram shows what happens when three holes are made in a plastic container of water.

3 Why does the water come out of the bottom hole fastest?
Tick **one** box.

Pressure is higher at the top. ☐

Pressure increases with depth in water. ☐

Pressure increases with temperature in water. ☐

The graph shows how the pressure in the air changes with height above the ground.

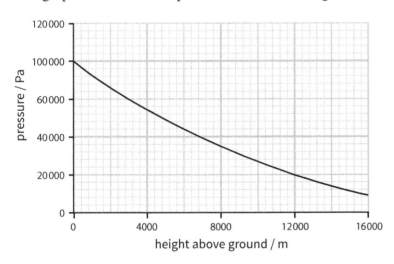

4 Describe the pattern shown in the graph.

....

....

5 What is the pressure at a height of 12 000 m above ground?

..............................Pa

6 At what height is the pressure 100 000 Pa?

....

> **Remember**
>
> Use the graph to work out your answers.

9.6 Moments

This exercise relates to **9.7 The turning effect of a force** and **9.8 The principle of moments** from the Coursebook.

> In this exercise, you make decisions about turning effects of forces.

Forces can make things turn.

The turning effect of a force is called a **moment**.

The fixed point about which an object turns is called the **pivot**.

Remember

- As the force increases, the moment increases.
- As the distance from the pivot increases, the moment increases.

Look at this example.

Nor is on her bicycle.

She pushes down on the pedal.

Nor's push is straight down, but it causes the chain wheel to turn. It produces a moment. The pivot is at the centre of the chain wheel. The pivot is always at the centre of the turn.

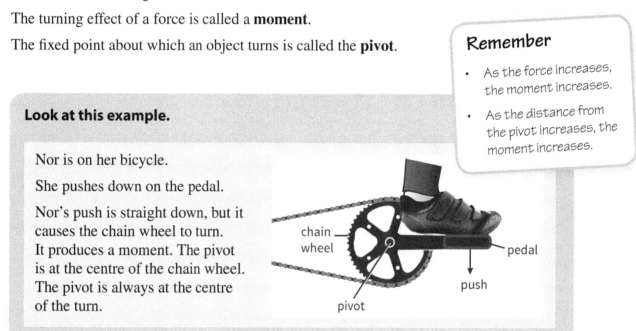

The diagram below shows a heavy door, seen from above.

Sam wants to push this door open.

He can push with a force of 100 N.

1 Which position, **A**, **B** or **C**, should he push to make the door open **most easily**? Tick **one** box.

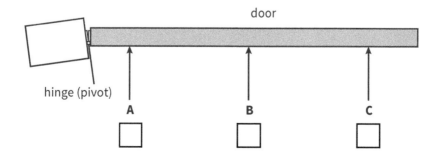

Elsa is investigating how different weights bend a long ruler.

She clamps the long ruler at one end so it can bend, as shown in the diagram.

table

long ruler

X

Elsa hangs different weights at point **X** at the other end of the ruler.

She measures how far the end of the ruler bends down each time.

The table shows her results.

Weight / N	How far the ruler bends down / cm
0	2.0
2	4.0
3	5.5
4	7.5

2 Complete the sentence:

As the weight gets larger, the ruler bends down ....

3 List **two** things that Elsa should keep constant during her investigation.

....

....

4 Elsa repeats the investigation using the **same** weights.

This time, she hangs them from position **Y**.

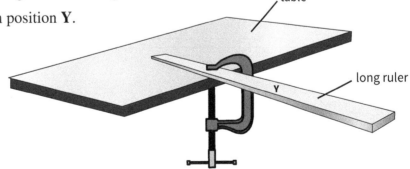

table

long ruler

Y

Explain how her results will be different this time.

....

....

10.1 Predicting effects of static electricity

This exercise relates to **10.1 Static electricity** and **10.2 Positive and negative charge** from the Coursebook.

> In this exercise, you predict what will happen when objects become charged.

Remember

When some objects are rubbed together, they become charged.

- **opposite** charges **attract**
- **like** charges **repel**.

1 Complete the sentences using words from the list.

like   **negative**   **neutral**   **positive**

Two objects rub together.

One object gains a positive charge. The other object gains a .... charge.

A negative charge will attract a .... charge.

2 Which of these is a result of static electricity?
   Tick **one** box.

clouds ☐   lightning ☐   rain ☐   wind ☐

Nor is investigating static electricity.

She hangs a small plastic ball on a piece of light string.

She knows that the ball has a **positive** charge.

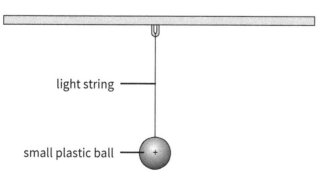

light string

small plastic ball

Nor rubs a plastic rod with a cloth.

She brings the plastic rod close to the ball.

The diagram shows the result.

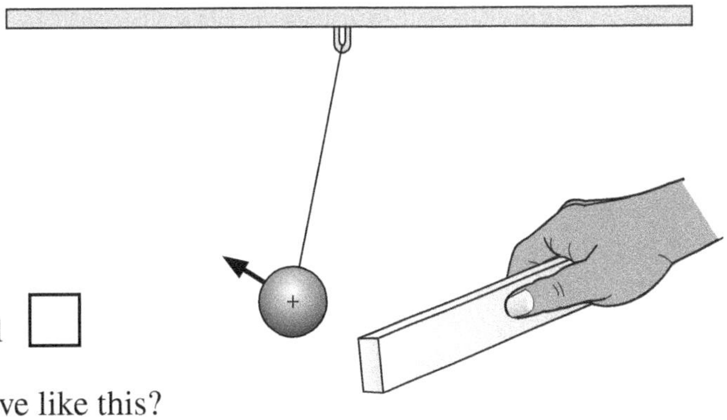

3 What is the charge on the **rod**?
Tick **one** box.

positive ☐   negative ☐   neutral ☐

4 What type of force causes the ball to move like this?
Draw a circle around **one** type of force.

contact   **non-contact**   **opposite**

Nor repeats the investigation.

She uses the same ball and the same rod.

This time, the rod has been rubbed for longer to give it a greater charge.

5 Complete the diagram to suggest what will happen to the ball this time.

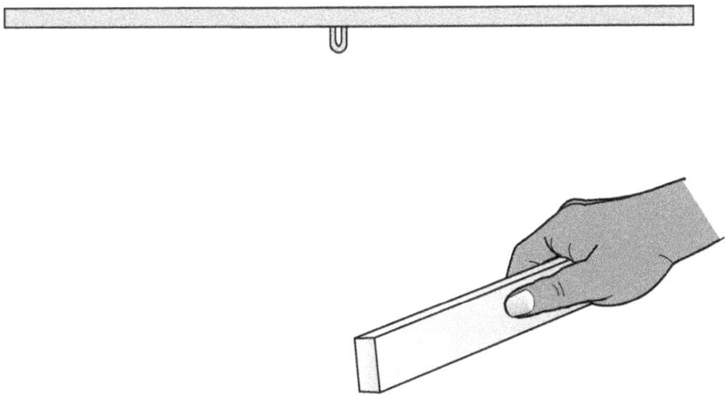

Nor then leaves the ball hanging on the string until the next day.

She rubs the **same rod** again to charge the rod.

She brings the rod up to the ball as before, but the ball does **not** move.

6 What has happened to the ball overnight?
Tick **one** box.

The ball has gained more charge.   ☐

The ball has gained an opposite charge.   ☐

The ball has lost its charge.   ☐

10.2 Conductors in circuits

This exercise relates to **10.4 Conductors and insulators** from the Coursebook.

> In this exercise, you decide whether objects are electrical conductors or insulators, and draw a circuit diagram.

Metals are conductors of electricity.

Non-metals are insulators. That means they do **not** conduct electricity.

Jon wants to investigate conductors and insulators.

He sets up the circuit shown below.

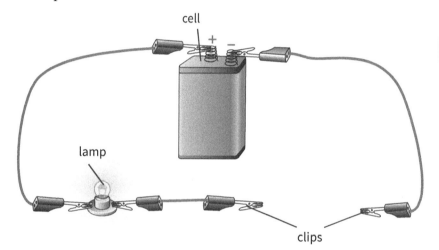

> **Remember**
>
> Electric current only flows in a complete circuit where all the parts are conductors.

Jon touches the clips together and the lamp lights.

1 Suggest why Jon does this **before** starting his investigation.

....

....

2 Jon puts some different materials between the clips, one at a time.

Complete the table to predict whether the lamp lights for each material.

The first two have been done for you.

Use a tick if the lamp will light, and a cross if it will **not** light.

Material	Does the lamp light?
copper wire	✓
plastic comb	✗
iron nail	
aluminium foil	
wooden ruler	
glass beaker	

3 Jon now removes the clips and connects the wires together so the lamp lights. Draw a circuit diagram for this circuit.

4 Which part of this circuit causes the current flow?
Tick **one** box.

battery ☐   lamp ☐   wires ☐

Some things need a more powerful supply of electricity than the battery on page 70. We plug them into wall sockets.

The pictures show some types of plugs that are used in different countries.

5 Complete the sentences about the plugs.

Choose words from the list. You can use each word once, more than once, or not at all.

conductor   insulator   metal   plastic   wood

The pins on the plugs are made from .... which is

a ....

The body of each plug is made from .... which is

an ....

The wire that comes from each plug is covered with ....

10.3 Measuring current

This exercise relates to **10.5 Electric current in a circuit** from the Coursebook.

> In this exercise, you think about the current in a circuit and how to measure it, and draw a graph.

Remember

A **series circuit** is one with no branches.

When a circuit is switched on, current flows.

Current is measured with an ammeter in the circuit.

The size of the current is the same the whole way round a series circuit.

1 The diagrams show three different ammeters.

Below each one, write down the current that the meter is showing.

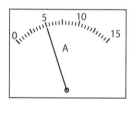 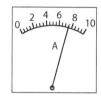 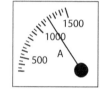

...............A   ....A   ....A

Elsa sets up the circuit shown in diagram **A** below.

The ammeter in circuit **A** reads 1.0 A.

She changes the order of the parts in the circuit, as shown in diagram **B**.

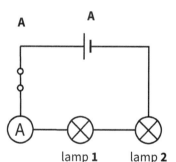 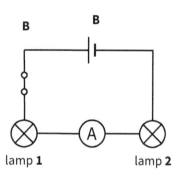

2 Write down the reading on the ammeter in circuit **B**. ....

3 Elsa **opens** the switch in circuit **B**. What will happen?
Tick **one** box.

Lamp 1 goes off before lamp 2.   ☐

Lamp 2 goes off before lamp 1.   ☐

Both lamps go off at the same time.   ☐

Nor is investigating how the number of lamps in a series circuit affects the current.

She sets up a circuit as shown in the diagram.

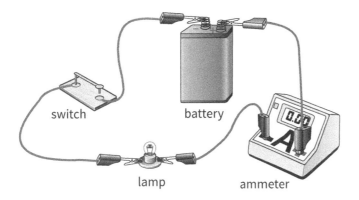

switch   battery

lamp   ammeter

4 Draw a circuit diagram for this circuit.

Nor records the current with one lamp in the circuit.

She then adds more lamps, one by one, in series.

She records the current each time.

Her results are shown in the table on the next page.

5 Plot Nor's results as a line graph on the grid below.

Draw a **smooth curve** through the points.

One of the results in the table does **not** fit the pattern. Your line does **not** have to pass through this point.

Remember

Choose your axis scales carefully.

Number of lamps	Current / A
1	2.0
2	1.0
3	0.9
4	0.5
5	0.4

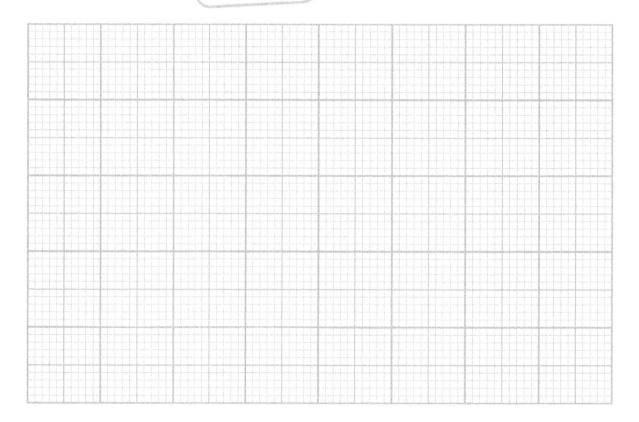

6 Describe the pattern in Nor's results.

....

....

....

7 Circle the result **on the graph** that does not fit the pattern.

How could Nor find out if this result is incorrect?

....

11.1 Displaying energy information

This exercise relates to **11.1 How we use energy** from the Coursebook.

> In this exercise, you decide on a way to represent and display data about energy use.

We can display information about energy use in various ways.

- Line graphs are used to show **continuous** variables.

- Bar charts are used to compare or show variables that are **not continuous**.

- Pie charts are used for information about **percentages**. The percentages add up to 100%.

The table shows how people in one country use energy in their homes in one year.

Energy used for	% of total energy used in home
heating rooms	42
other uses	24
heating water	18
cooling rooms	6
lighting	5
refrigeration	5

1 State the best way to display this information.

....

Give a reason for your choice.

....

....

2 Suggest what type of weather this country has for most of the year.
Tick **one** box and give a reason for your choice.

cold weather ☐   hot weather ☐

Reason:

....

....

3 The table lists 'other uses'. Suggest **two** other energy uses in the home.

....

....

Some new electrical items have an energy rating.

Items are rated from A to G. An item rated 'A' uses the least energy and an item rated 'G' uses the most energy.

An example for an item rated 'A' is shown.

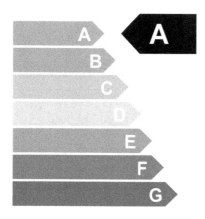

4 What type of information display is this energy rating diagram?
Tick **one** box.

bar chart ☐   line graph ☐   pie chart ☐

5 Suggest **one** reason for displaying the energy rating on electrical items.

....

....

6 Global use of energy is increasing every year.

Sam finds a table on the internet that gives global energy use every year from 2005 to 2015.

Suggest the best way to display this information.

....

Give a reason for your choice.

....

7 Write down **one** reason why global energy use is increasing.

....

....

11.2 Looking at different energy sources

This exercise relates to **11.3 Renewables and non-renewables** from the Coursebook.

> In this exercise, you draw and interpret different types of graphs showing information about energy sources.

We can group energy sources as two types:

- **non-renewable** – fossil fuels (coal, oil and natural gas) and nuclear fuel
- **renewable** – wind, water, solar and biofuel.

1 Describe what is meant by:

a a non-renewable energy source.

....

b a renewable energy source.

....

2 Oil is a fossil fuel.

What type of useful energy is stored in oil? Tick **one** box.

chemical ☐   electrical ☐

nuclear ☐   thermal ☐

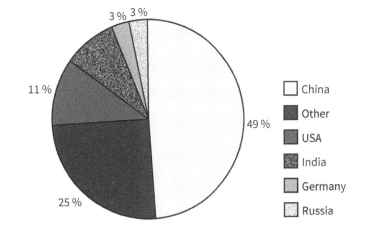

3 The pie chart shows which countries use the largest percentages of the world's coal.

Use information in the pie chart to answer these questions.

a Which country uses the most coal? ....

b What percentage of the world's coal does the USA use? ....

c Work out what percentage of the world's coal is used by India.

Show how you worked out your answer.

....

....

Solar panels can be used to generate electricity using energy from the Sun.
Elsa is investigating the power output of a solar panel.

She puts a solar panel outside on a sunny day.
She lays the solar panel flat on the ground.

She leaves the solar panel outside from
before sunrise until after sunset.

The diagram shows her investigation.

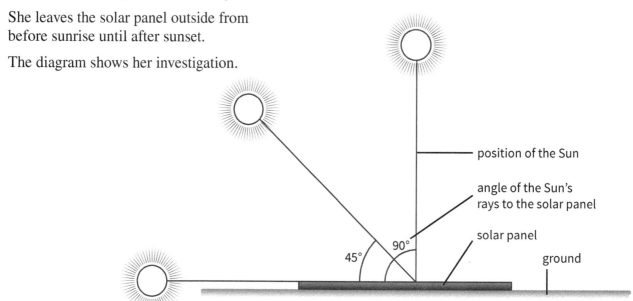

4 What type of energy is solar energy?
   Draw a circle around one word.

   electrical   chemical   renewable

5 The sun rises at 06:00. At this time, the angle of the sun's rays
   to Elsa's solar panel is 0°.

   Suggest the time of day she recorded her last result at 90°.

   ....

Elsa measures the power output of the solar panel
for different angles between 0° and 90°.

The table shows her results.

Angle of the Sun's rays to the solar panel /degrees	Power output /W
0	2.4
15	5.6
30	7.8
45	9.6
60	10.8
75	11.8
90	12.0

6 Draw a line graph of Elsa's results on the grid below.

- Use a scale of 1 cm to 10° on the *x*-axis.
- Use a scale of 1 cm to 1 W on the *y*-axis.
- Draw a smooth curve through your points.

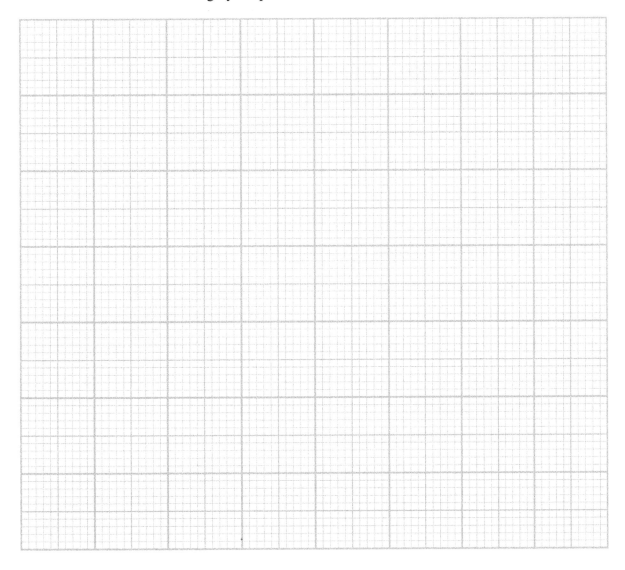

7 Describe the pattern in Elsa's results.

....

....

8 Suggest what the power output of Elsa's solar panel would be at night.

....

11.3 Investigating heat conduction

This exercise relates to **11.4 Conduction of heat** from the Coursebook.

> In this exercise, you make predictions about the conduction of heat.

Nor is investigating heat conduction.

She uses wax to attach paper clips to a copper rod.

She heats one end of the copper rod. She records the time taken for the paper clips to fall off.

heat   wax   copper rod

paper clip

1 On the diagram, draw a circle around the paper clip that will fall off first.

2 Complete the sentence below using a word from this list.

condenses   freezes   melts   evaporates

The paper clips fall off because the wax ………………………………… .

3 Nor then repeats the experiment using a glass rod.

Write down **three** things that Nor needs to keep the same when comparing the glass rod with the copper rod.

………………………………………………………………………………………………………

………………………………………………………………………………………………………

………………………………………………………………………………………………………

4 It took 4 minutes for all the paper clips to fall off the copper rod.

How will the time compare for the glass rod?
Tick **one** box.

It will be shorter. ☐

It will be longer. ☐

It will be the same. ☐

> **Remember**
>
> Metals are good conductors of heat (thermal conductors).
>
> Non-metals are not good conductors of heat. Non-metals make good thermal insulators.

5 Nor wants to repeat the experiment with a plastic rod.

Write down why Nor will **not** be able to collect any results with the plastic rod.

………………………………………………………………………………………………………